THE DENNIS DOHERTY STORY

the inspiration for the Sound and Light Show of Norfolk Island

June Allen

Kwizzel ®

Publishing

86A Lynn Rd, Bayview, Auckland NZ 0629

I express appreciation to Michael Prentice of Pine Tree Tours who devised the Sound and Light Show, and commissioned me to research and write the script. The production opened in 1984 and has long been a very popular tourist attraction on Norfolk Island.

Grateful thanks are also due to the late Margaret Hazzard for her encouragement and historical advice, to David Lewis who wrote the ship arrival scene, and the opening dialogue of the Bloody Bridge scene, to the late Karl and Kathy Davies, former proprietors of the Bounty Museum, and to the Norfolk Island library for allowing me to search their historical records.

Special thanks to my friend, the late Nicholas Porter, for insisting I publish this story, to Professor John Dunmore for his eagle eye in proof reading, and to Bev Robitai for guiding me through the publishing process.

June Allen

FULL COLOUR EDITION
ISBN 978-0-473-27064-3

The rattle of chains,

a groan;

prisoners tramp

through sticky mud.

The lash ….

the lash ….

"Give 'im three 'undred!"

FOREWORD

Norfolk Island is a dot in the South Pacific, a tiny island 8 km by 5 km. There was no recorded habitation on the island before Captain James Cook set foot in 1774. However, his crew found rows of bananas which indicated an earlier settlement, no doubt by Melanesians en route during fishing expeditions. Cook had seen the island while sailing to New Zealand, and reported to the English government that the massive trees he saw, now known as Norfolk pines, would be ideal for ships' masts. England was rebuilding her navy after the destructive wars against the French and this was good news. However, it turned out that pine trunks were not suitable, for there are too many knots in the grain, and the timber is quite soft.

King George III recognized that the island would be useful, however; and did not want it falling into the hands of the French who were also exploring that part of the Pacific. George III decreed therefore, on arrival of the First Fleet in Botany Bay in January 1788, that a boatload of trusted convicts and some free men, tradesmen, should travel to the tiny island. They were directed to form a settlement before the French could take possession of the island.

Lieutenant Philip Gidley King and his tiny band of settlers travelled more than a thousand miles from New South Wales to found the First Settlement on Norfolk Island in 1788. Lieutenant King was therefore the first Superintendent of Norfolk Island.

It was not many years later that this island became known as 'The Hell-hole of the Pacific". Recalcitrant offenders from Port Arthur in Tasmania, and those frequently attempting escape from that prison, were sent to Norfolk Island.

Their incorrigible behaviour, and that of many commandants and officers, changed the island from a peaceful settlement to one where the most extreme measures of punishment were carried out.

By 1814 the treatment of prisoners had become so vile that the prison was closed down. Buildings of the First Settlement had been built of timber and these were burnt to the ground in an effort to expunge the horror. All those living on the island returned to New South Wales.

Despite this earlier experience, eleven years later, in 1825, another attempt was made to develop an escape proof prison for repeat offenders.

This new prison became known as the Second Settlement, and the buildings were constructed of stone.

Needless to say, the officers who administered the prison, and the wives who accompanied them, were also affected by the dreadful isolation.

Many buildings of the Second Settlement have been faithfully restored after an Archeological Survey by Graham Wilson and Martin Davies for the Australian Commonwealth Department of Housing and Construction.

These buildings, rich in history, were the stimulus for the Dennis Doherty story which forms the basis for the Sound and Light Show of Norfolk Island. It is a stark reminder of brutal days on Norfolk Island.

This is not a chronological account, but rather a blend of recorded happenings during both the First and Second Settlements on Norfolk Island.

THE DENNIS DOHERTY STORY

The narrator of the Sound and Light Show is Dennis Doherty who was a real person; all the incidents in the story portrayed in the show were taken from historical records. In some instances chronology was altered to enhance the narrative.

At the commencement of the tour, the coach takes the traveller from the township of Burnt Pine, down Taylors Road towards Kingston, earlier called Sydneytown.

But wait; there is a brief stop on the way. After twisting down through the area known as Windmill, the driver stops and opens the coach door. 'Come aboard', he says.

It seems that in the darkness the driver has seen a passenger waiting at the side of the road. It's after dark, the interior light hasn't been turned on and it's difficult to see if indeed we've been joined by another passenger. Was there really anyone waiting?

Perhaps it is the ghost of Dennis Doherty. We hear a voice, it is that of an old man. The voice pervades the interior of the coach and we realise we are to hear a story of long ago. Sixty years may not be very old by modern standards, but this is the voice of a man who has seen many deaths, and has been subject to many punishments – horrors you could not imagine.

In the darkness we begin to hear his story. There is desperation and bitterness in his voice, but the soft and seductive tones of an Irish brogue are still there.

"Friends; my name is Dennis Doherty. It is only a hundred and sixty years ago that I was living in this hell-hole called Norfolk Island. Yes, the Ocean Hell. Do you not hear the sounds? There are fifteen hundred convicts on this island now. Can't you hear them working?"

Through the still night air comes the muffled sound of hammer on chisel breaking rock, rock falling, a man's howl of pain, and the groans of men suffering terrible trauma.

Doherty continues his story: "Those of us who were too smart for the guards in Van Diemen's Land were transported to this tiny island. There is no worse place for His Majesty's subjects than the prison on Norfolk Island."

There is a slow, grating, metallic sound – men dragging leg irons, the vicious crack of a whip, and a man's awful cry as the lashes strike his back.

"I have only one good eye, and I wear the skull and cross-bones tattooed on my arm." Thus Dennis Doherty describes himself. "I feel like an old man now, but bear with me. I have such a story to tell you. I've been forty-two years in Australian prisons, and had three thousand lashes over that time. These swine have almost broken me.

I crave to see once more the gentle green hills of dear Derry in blessed Ireland from whence I came so long ago.

As I speak to you now, it seems an age since I was a young man, not more than fourteen years old, when I was first sentenced to prison. That was for deserting the ranks of the 16th Lancers.

When a young man is exposed to the violence of prison life of more than a hundred and sixty years before your time, gentle readers, you can well believe how his personality is debased and warped. This hardening of a man's very being was the only way to survive and keep some sort of reason.

I am one of the incorrigibles who was sent from prison in Van Diemen's land, where I had been in heavy irons in the quarry gang. I had been accused of being a ringleader, and king of the rebels. So it is hardly surprising that I, being a natural rebel, try to break out of any gaol they lock me into?

I have tried to escape – always that dream of escaping haunts me – as a bird does from its cage. Is that so unnatural? Is that dream such a great crime?

Those of us who have endured the rigorous discipline and flogging in other prisons in New South Wales and Van Diemen's Land, have since been subjected to unheard-of cruelties on Norfolk Island. The degradation we suffered in this place lowered us to the very depths of despair.

When I refused to work I was beaten again, and left with only bread and water for weeks on end. A lesser man would have died. I wasn't going to give the bastards that satisfaction!

For having a hat – yes, merely a hat – in my possession, I was given a sentence of three months hard labour in chains. To be found with tobacco in my possession was deserving of fourteen days in solitude.

The guards would search our mouths with their filthy fingers, at any time of day or night, yes – even wake us from our sleep – looking for traces of tobacco. I have spent two weeks in solitary often because of my craving for the stuff.

What other pleasure does a real man have? We can't get to the liquor that is locked in the store … believe me we've dreamed of it … and the only other earthly pleasure a man could have is deprived us in this prison of only men. Well … many do compromise. They need sex – still have the energy, remarkably so – and have had their pleasure in, what the Reverend politely calls, 'unnatural offences'.

I have much to tell you this evening. Sit back in your comfortable horseless carriage, but don't get too comfortable because – I have a tale to unfold of times less than two hundred years ago when this island was a dreaded hell for thousands like myself."

The coach reaches Kingston Pier and to the west, in the fading light we see the ocean heaving, and spray from the never ceasing waves that crash against the cliffs.

Doherty's voice invades the peace. "Let us go and watch the good ship, *The Governor Phillip*, being discharged of her most recent cargo.

The prisoners arriving have earlier come from the slums of England. Most were first detained in the rotting ship hulks that littered the Thames and other rivers on England's southern coast. The ships that transported them halfway across the world could only be described as floating dungeons.

Most of the men who came on that interminable journey were in double irons. The filth and vermin that surrounded and encased them, so many human bodies being crowded together in the holds, cannot be imagined by decent souls such as yourselves."

Lone pine on Point Hunter with Nepean and Phillip Islands in the background

SCENE ONE:
KINGSTON PIER

The sounds of yesteryear invade the listeners' senses. In the darkness we realise that a ship is just offshore, its timbers creaking, and canvas sails cracking in the wind.

Across the rocks at Kingston at low tide

The ship's mate yells instructions, and the voice of the captain can also be heard in the ensuing din. He's shouting instructions to the coxswain throughout the manoeuvre. The ship must negotiate the narrow channel between the reef and the cliffs.

"All hands on deck!"
"Two points to starboard, Cox'n."

"Three fathoms water under the keel, Sir."

"Two chain to go."

"Haul in the mainsail!"

"Two fathoms under the keel."

"Stand by the boats! Look lively on those ropes, lads. Stand by the anchor!"

"Two fathoms on rock, Sir."

"Let go anchors!"

"Anchors aweigh, Cap'n"

The sails have been hauled, and the anchor drops with a huge splash and jabs into the sandy bottom as the ship lurches between the heaving waves and the rocks.

"Quartermaster! Open the prisoners' hatch."

"Aye, aye, sir. Come on, ye foul smellin' vermin. Here's ye new home – Norfolk Island. This may well be yer last restin' place. Ha ha!"

There is the rumble of a timber hatch being rolled open, and the babble of voices of the prisoners who have travelled for more than a week crowded in the hold.

The quartermaster yells: "Keep silence below! McManus, unshackle the prisoners; they may have to swim. Come on, me beauties; behold Norfolk Island! May God have mercy on you, for sure no-one else will. Step lively up the ladder, me fine gentlemen. The Major has a welcome for ye ashore."

His laugh is bitter.

"Lower the boats."

"Move along, you scum – first dozen into the longboat. Look sharp!"

"Bring the next lot up."

"Stand aside for the officer, you prisoners!"

Dennis Doherty takes up the narrative. "The old hands among the convicts were eager to see what their new fellow prisoners would be like. Those already on the island were quick to take advantage of any situation, and often stole precious belongings that the latest arrivals might have hidden and brought with them.

There are one hundred and twenty arriving today. Can you hear their bewildered voices?"

The convicts are in a confused state as they struggle onto the ship's deck and then are bullied ashore.

"I can't see clearly. The sunlight's too bright after bein' barricaded below decks for so long."
"What is this place? Where have the bastards brought us?"
"The two men who were convicted with me will never see the light of day again. They died of cholera on the journey out."
"It's warmer than old Blighty, anyway."

The camp overseer ashore barks his orders. "Sergeant, march these thugs to the Goal without delay."

A voice screams, "Help! Somebody wait – help me over the rocks! My chain has become caught and this dangerous tide is terrifying!"

Doherty speaks again. His voice is still calm. He has become inured to these ghastly conditions. "All the convicts were finally landed on shore, though as time passes many of them will wish for an easy end. It would have been better if they had perished on the journey here."

SCENE TWO:
THE BOATSHED

The tour turns now towards the old boatshed by the pier. It was replastered and painted in the early 1980s by the Australian Government and now looks much as it did in Doherty's time.

Dennis Doherty tells of convict times in the old buildings at Kingston. "Let's listen to the voices of the men who worked and slaved in the buildings that surround you.

Over there on the right you see the boatshed. This is always locked and guarded at night to prevent the convicts stealing a boat and trying to make their escape at sea. Many a winter's night it was cold and miserable down here. The guards hated this lonely watch."

The boatshed

An officer takes us back in time. "I am Officer Barney, and I am responsible for the security of the boats locked away in this shed. There are two launches of about ten ton each, and two six-oared whaleboats, housed in this building.

The old sheds that we used before have become dilapidated, and the prisoners have made several attempts to break through the doors and take the boats. How far they would manage to escape is uncertain, but the fools are desperate enough to try anything. The chances of survival at sea are almost nil, of course, but some of the prisoners would prefer to take even that slim chance of escape."

SCENE THREE:
THE ROYAL ENGINEERS OFFICE

The light from the tour coach now shines on a beautifully restored building, which in modern times is used as the Administration tour office. William Riley stands outside.

Doherty carries on, "Now to the Royal Engineers Office. This is the work place of the clerks responsible for planning the construction of the buildings that are around Kingston."

A military officer speaks in clipped, correct English. "We need able bodied men from England to build this settlement. We will also need skilled stonemasons for cutting the stone into blocks. Thousands of yards of stone must be quarried. The convicts will be employed every day at Point Hunter until this has been achieved."

Dennis Doherty speaks again. "The convicts, as well as enlisted men, did the work. The preliminary construction was done in the lumber yard and under strict supervision.

This was a place where the most vicious of the convict overseers used, and abused, their power. An overseer chosen from the convict population usually turned out to be far more cruel towards his fellow inmates than the officers.

The best stone for building was that taken from just below high water mark at Point Hunter, and from Nepean Island. It is plain to see, stone that has over the years been subjected to waves and currents, would be worn smooth."

The convict standing on the lawn in front of the Engineers Office speaks. "My name is William Riley. Life has become easier for me now, though I am still a convict of the Crown. I have suffered like my fellow countryman, Dennis Doherty, but thank God, not as long as he has. Mind you, I once had fifty lashes across my back for the dubious crime of insolence. And I have spent five years and two months in leg irons.

But they have tamed me at last, and as I stand before you now I have as good a position as any prisoner could hope for while still being on Norfolk Island. I am proud to tell you that I am now the overseer in the Engineers' Department. They have recognized my worth at last."

SCENE FOUR:
THE CRANKMILL

The light fades on Riley, and behind us we hear cries and groans from men working on the crankmill. The crankmill is a tall building, in earlier times three storeys high.

There is the sound of stone grinding mercilessly on stone, and creaking from rough iron cogs.

Doherty introduces the viewer to the memories that cry out in this inhuman place. "On your left is the crankmill. Don't think for a moment that the purpose of this building was solely to grind meal for the prison.

In fact, the wheat and maize was usually ground at the water mill. The crankmill was designed to be a punishment for the men in irons, and cruel punishment it was, indeed."

We hear the screams of men in pain; screeching, moaning and yelling in desperation.

A convict yells, "Quick. Pull on this section now! Jerk it loose …. that's right! They won't be able to fix till the morning. We'll have some rest from this bloody heat and pain."

The voices cry out again; shouting, whistling, yelling, hooting and swearing.

The crank mill ruins seen from the convict hospital

Doherty: "See these men, begrimed – dirt and sweat – glaring madness in their eyes. The crank was poorly designed, but who cares? Tremendous exertion is needed to move it round. Thank God that Commandant Bunbury did not have his way, or we would be walking the treadmill as well.

A hundred convicts at a time work in this tall building; they move just as a chain pump does in a man-o-war ship.

Those of you who know of the noise and confusion on the gun decks in the midst of wartime action will have some realization of the dizzying heat and turmoil in this mill."

SCENE FIVE:
THE NEW GAOL

The bus moves around to view 'The New Gaol', always known as such because it replaced an earlier one. The impressive arched gateway almost twenty feet high, set in massive stone walls, is the backdrop for the following scene.

The gates of the New Gaol.

Doherty: "Captain Alexander Maconochie, the great prison reformer, was relieved of his duties in 1844 because, in the opinion of his superiors, he had let discipline within the prison become far too lax. Commandant Childs took over from Maconochie.

The old hands amongst the prisoners believed they could get away with almost anything because of Commandant Maconochie's good marks system. Hope of easier conditions had been filtering through to the newly arrived convicts.

However, prisoners who spent their early years in the revolting conditions of London slum areas were hardened criminals. The flogging that was handed out daily by Major Anderson during his term as commandant, and others, seemed to have little effect on them."

Doherty continues: "One of the most remarkable buildings of the Second Settlement was built under Commandant Child's command."

The sound of chisels chipping on stone as hundreds of tons of rock are formed into huge building blocks are the background to this description.

"The work of building this new gaol was already behind schedule when Childs arrived on Norfolk Island to take command.

It was not foreseen that the prison settlement would be shut down forever after just fourteen years.

Commandant Major Childs ordered that a pentagonal prison be constructed. There were to be underground cells for the worst offenders. We dreaded the solitary darkness even more than the lash. This was the only major building task under Child's command."

Some convicts can be heard muttering and complaining amongst themselves. Most voices have rough London accents.

"Why can't we have more meat?"
"All the best meat goes to the hospital."
"It's too late to help the men who are in there."
"We are suffering from dysentery ….."
"…. from eating this foul ….."
"…. and tough salt beef."

"Always salt beef.

In the First Settlement the men managed to escape at night and ran through the bush to Mt Pitt where they caught birds. They were the only ones who had a change from the wretched salt beef."

"But they were so exhausted the next day that it hardly seemed worth the trouble. Which is worse? Lack of sleep, or lack of food?"

"It's not just the stale meat which gives us this ghastly dysentery; it's eleven hundred prisoners sleeping at close quarters, and disease spreads like wildfire."

"Yes. But you soon realize that those of us who have been here the longest have most resistance. It's the new hands just out from England who are dying like flies."

With a menacing chuckle he adds, "It's a good thing that we helped ourselves to their precious belongings when they arrived. They have little use for them now."

"There are always plenty more on the next ship to take their place."

"When the next boat comes from Port Jackson with stores I'll be part of the crew which unloads her. I'll risk the 'cat' for the sake o' the chance to get away from this hell-hole. It's the likes of the flogging triangle, and the Cyclian gag that has a man frothing at the mouth and gurgling blood, which have earned this place the name of the Ocean Hell."

Doherty urges them to stop. "Look! Here comes Commander Childs towards us. Whisper now so that he doesn't hear you."

The men see Commander Childs move forward from the prison gate, as he barks an order. "Have stone quarried from Point Hunter for this building."

First Officer, "Aye, aye, Sir."

Commandant Childs, "The biggest blocks cut from Nepean Island will be needed for masonry at the grand entrance. Ensure that those convicts that go across to the island are ironed so that there is no chance of their escaping.

We have seventeen hundred convicts in our charge, and there is some risk of revolt. That man, Kavanagh, and his followers must be watched particularly."

Kavanagh mutters, "I heard that! That pompous up fellow from the old country will learn a thing or two about us outlaws from Tasmania. He should watch out for Dennis Doherty, methinks I smell trouble."

The bus moves on slowly, the spotlight fades but voices can still be heard recounting the horrors of incarceration. A prisoner speaks. "I'm going to knock off a sheep tonight. This is driving me crazy, not having fresh meat. I won't bear it any longer."

Doherty: "He crept up by the light of the waning moon and found an animal – one that was easy to catch – an old ewe - but one that would be good as fresh tucker for a week or more. One of the wardens heard the man though, and shouted out, ordering him to halt."

The prisoner carries on, "That was the last call the warden made in his wretched life. No way was I going to allow him to keep me from my fresh meat. Not when I'd got so near it! Not after I'd struggled for months to keep alive, suffering heavy, punishing work from dawn to dusk, only fed on Indian flour and weevily infested wheat. And always the wretched salt beef. It would be better to chew old leather!"

Another prisoner speaks. "When the warden tried to stop my mate, he turned and cut him down fast. The other guards found their companion the next day. His stomach had been split open, and what d'ye think was hanging out? Why, the sheep's guts, of course." He chortles with glee at the memory.

Doherty continues, "We slept here, eleven hundred of us in this gaol alone; in hammocks slung in double tiers. Oh, the unbelievable squalor of the Old Gaol: so many men always in irons; night and day those accursed irons. They were so heavily manacled that their legs were permanently ulcerous. You may consider Major Childs a cruel man, but there is even worse of our history to relate.

Commandant Price brought horror of a hitherto unheard-of degree. He had an unnerving habit of staring through his monocle and taunting the men, daring them to speak back. The law was: if prisoners so much as raise their voices in self-defence they were to be given the lash.

John Price, of all the commandants on Norfolk Island, bred so much hatred that, when he was later the Inspector General of Convicts in Victoria, his maddened victims murdered him most horribly."

SCENE SIX:
THE TORTURES

As the tour coach winds slowly along the waterfront road, three tableaux in succession are lit up. Turn your head away if you don't want to see the horror of flogging, and worse. Dennis Doherty's voice comes close to breaking point as he describes the instruments of torture that were used.

The first tableau depicts the Spreadeagle. A dummy likeness of a prisoner has its arms spread widely, and is hung against the stone wall of the New Gaol so that its feet dangle almost two metres from the ground.

The overseer's voice comes through the gloom in vicious tones. "His crime deserves no less than the spreadeagle."

Doherty says, "We all knew it was against the regulations, but the villains in command would hang a man this way for up to five hours at a time. They thought that if we witnessed his agony it might make us mend our ways. Nay; it only made us hate them more."

The light fades, the bus moves on and the spotlight fixes on a scourge (whiphand) preparing to use the lash on a convict tied to a huge wooden triangle. Doherty spits out his words in disgust. He builds to fever pitch. "The favourite pastime of all the military guards was nicknamed 'going to the races'. What a meanly phrased term to describe watching the pain of those who suffered the lash, and no doubt watching with glee.

Oh, my God; how bitterly I remember it. No-one had ever less than fifty lashes. I have even known of men being given three hundred lashes before breakfast. The scourge would beat a man's back till he could see the bone. The doctors should never have allowed things like that to happen, but some of them were sadists, too."

The flogging proceeds. We hear the whip crack, a man moaning, and a voice counting persistently, "One hundred and three, one hundred and four, one hundred and five" …. the voice increases in intensity, in excitement, unremitting …. "one hundred and twenty one, one hundred and twenty two," and can be heard till the light fades.

Dennis Doherty: "The sound of 'the cat' on naked flesh is like a horse whip – the sound gnaws into your mind and into your spirit."

Voices of convicts call out in desperation, "The souls of the dead are screaming for vengeance."

A military officer yells orders. "Give that man two hundred lashes."

Doherty: "I was given two hundred lashes last week for neglect of work and disgusting language, if you please. Two hundred lashes! I'll use whatever language want!"

We are treated worse than the rats that scuttle through the store. I have had the lash so often that I have lost count. Huh! Would you believe that there was the time I had fifty lashes for trading my bed and blanket? That turned out to be no fair trade indeed!"

More voices: "After I was flogged, I was put in fifty pound irons and manacles. That was tortuous pain. I couldn't rest, whatever position I took."

"The ants are carrying away the flesh from my mate's back that was left on the bloodied triangle."

"The blood flowed in rivers."

"On some mornings the ground where the poor buggers stood at the triangle was saturated with human gore, as if a bucket of blood and scraps of flesh had been spilt across it."

The light fades, but memories of the voices are still with us.

Doherty has more to tell. "Commandant Price was the man who really relished the use of the lash. He would stare through his monocle with cold unconcern as the punishment was carried out.

There was one bastard of a scourge that I remember who was so carried away by the thrill of his task, that he finished the count of two hundred lashes, even though his victim had become a corpse some minutes before."

The voice of an older, truly broken man joins in. "I am the spirit of William Castleton. Though I was an old man I was given a flogging sentence. My wretched body didn't survive the punishment. My spirit left the mortal world."

Lights come up on the third torture scene. It is the last in this sequence, and perhaps you have seen enough already. There is a man chained with his ankle connecting his wrist, thus forcing him into a continual crouching position.

Doherty: "Here is another suffering from the weird tortures that were dreamt up by our satanic guards. A man, though chained like this, was still ordered to work all day in the blazing sun. Some have died while chained like this."

There is a quicker way to die. The bus pulls up beside the Gallows Gate. There is a Military guard, and a padre, standing by. Ironically, the settlement believes in the sanctity of a man's soul after death, though most often he has been reduced to an inhuman state whilst alive and imprisoned on Norfolk Island.

A convict prepares to take his final walk.

Dennis Doherty speaks, "There was a merciful release from the prison on Norfolk Island. The first hanging of the Second Penal Settlement was in 1834."

The padre's voice is heard. "Lord God on high. We plead before Your throne of Mercy, that You extend to this, your faithful servant, remission of his sins, and divine grace."

Other voices join in the prayer. "Our Father, who art in Heaven…"

While the prayer is intoned, the military guard mounts the steps to the platform. He fastens a noose around the man's neck. The lever squeaks up, the trap springs open, and then there is darkness as the body drops.

Doherty continues, "The most ghastly event was when twelve men were hanged on one morning, after the judge delivered a mass sentence. The men had been found guilty together of a mutinous uprising in September 1834. They were executed, in the manner you have just witnessed, in two batches of six. The rest of us prisoners were marshalled into the compound to watch as our comrades thrashed out their last few minutes of life on this earth, dangling from the ropes.

It was His Honour, Fielding Brown, who had the heartlessness to dispose of so many human lives in this way. Following the hanging, the twelve bodies were trundled along the road, and flung into an open grave outside the cemetery's consecrated ground. More of that story later.

This was not the only occasion of mass slaughter of human life. At another time seventeen men were hanged in the short space of just seven weeks."

SCENE SEVEN:
THE HOSPITAL

The convict hospital

The coach turns. It follows the road along the beachfront at Slaughter Bay, and comes to a stop outside the ruins of the old hospital.

Doherty: "There is more to see yet, my friends. We will call on the surgeon at the Civil Hospital."

The spotlight picks out the figure of the surgeon standing at the top of the steps. He is resplendent in grey morning coat, just the thing for a morning's surgery, and holds a scalpel – or is it a carpenter's saw? – and a cloth dripping with blood.

There is a more than a hint of sarcasm in Doherty's voice as he continues. "Let's hear what the good doctor has to say. Forgive him if he rambles at times. He was a sane man when he arrived at the settlement, but he has been driven to drink, as have others before him, by what he must do."

The surgeon speaks. "I was trained to treat sick bodies, but I am appalled by the battered and torn bodies that reach me here from the prison. They are truly terrible to see.

Often the flesh is torn from the men's backs, and some have been whipped and flogged so often that they are brutalized and seem not to be able to suffer further degradation.
Then there are those who have suffered because of the shocking food and utter lack of hygiene. If they have the cursed dysentery that affects so many of the new arrivals after their sea voyage, they do not stand an even chance of surviving.

When this building was planned, those responsible quite overlooked the need for a kitchen, or even a morgue. So in order to accommodate these and a dispensary, there are now only four wards. In each of these wards are ten pallet mattresses on low iron beds.

There is never enough fresh bedding, and the wind whistles through here in all seasons. I cannot blame my patients for complaining of the bitter cold in winter, and excessive heat in summer."

Doherty: "It was even worse in days gone by. This building was only erected ten years before my time. Previously, a straw hut had been the only shelter for sick convicts."

The surgeon speaks again. "Smell the terrible stench from the privy. It seems that I am under sentence myself because of these conditions. Yet there are some prisoners who choose to spend their days in hospital rather than out working on the chain gang. Sadly, it is my duty to report any malingering, and the punishments are harsh for this offence. I have seen one man given two hundred lashes for malingering.

The last Commandant here, John Price, had the answer, or so he believed, for any convict who might try to use the hospital for a refuge for a period. Price decreed that if a man was too sick to work, then he was too sick to eat! My patients were starving!"

The doctor returns to his grisly business of amputation, and the light fades.

SCENE EIGHT:
THE COMMISSARIAT STORE

Before the coach reaches the store, Doherty has time to explain some of the historical background of this part of penal settlement life. "The two magnificent buildings which we are approaching were constructed under the direction of Commandant Anderson. He concentrated his efforts on these two establishments during his time on Norfolk Island.

The first one we'll see is the Commissariat Store. It is still one of the biggest buildings on Norfolk Island, and has walls three feet thick. It took two months to excavate and level that part of the hill behind, and eight months to complete building.

Timber cut from the surrounding hills was used for the bearers; Norfolk Island pines, of course.

The whole is a fine example of Georgian architecture.

This new store was designed to replace two former smaller buildings that were nearer the waterfront. Those had often been flooded by storms and raging spring tides. The ceiling of the lower storey of this Commissariat Store has been removed now, but the basement remains."

A light comes up showing the steps of the store, an overseer standing at the top. He says, "It is my duty to keep stock of the tools that the convicts use both in the fields and for cutting stone. You can expect some of them will try to chisel through their leg irons during the day whilst working.

Our guards will check the irons on each man – and if there are signs that there have been attempts to cut through, then that convict will be flogged. Any man who returns damaged tools at the end of the day will also face a flogging!"

Dennis Doherty: "The tools condemned as no longer being serviceable were thrown into the blowhole not far from Kingston pier, from where there is no possibility of their being recovered and used by the prisoners for nefarious purposes. The store also houses liquor for the guards and officers. Look! Here comes a convict now, in from the fields with the sack of grain that he's harvested. It will be stored on the upper floor."

The overseer indicates with a wave of his hand that the convict is to mount the steps. Two military guards supervise proceedings. The overseer inspects what the convict has in the huge pack slung over his shoulders, indicates his approval and the convict disappears into the Store.

Darkness falls. Doherty resumes his tale: "Let's move further along this road at Kingston to the New Military Barracks."

SCENE NINE:
THE NEW MILITARY BARRACKS

"This fine building was erected in addition to the Old Barracks, and was occupied by the unmarried soldiers. It is a much stronger building than the Old Barracks in all respects. To keep it well clear of the swampy ground, the convicts working on this project were forced to excavate part of the hill to three hundred and thirty feet in depth, and seven hundred feet in length.

After the successful completion of the Commissariat Store, Major Anderson's plans and specifications were approved for these New Barracks. Their construction took much longer than the Store, a total of two years and two months."

The coach draws up under the arched gateway of the Barracks. There is a group of soldiers to be seen, drinking and playing cards on the wide verandah. They begin to tussle amongst themselves. They're drunk and rowdy – it's their evening off duty.

The new military barracks

Doherty: "Oh, those bloody, drunken guards. Most of them were prisoners within themselves. Yet there were compensations for them in this life on Norfolk Island; they could enjoy swimming in the lagoon, and go fishing. These were pleasant pastimes for a free man.

Although there is liquor shipped here for their consumption, its arrival is erratic and the cost high. So they make a powerful brew from the wild lemons that grow all across the island.

Rabbits and goats were brought out from England. These animals were let loose on Phillip Island so that the officers and soldiers could enjoy shooting, as in the Old Country. No thought was given to what destruction of vegetation there would be. The rabbits bred like ... well, like rabbits! Phillip Island was soon barren and remained that way till the mid 1990s.

These men also had huge dogs to keep us wretched prisoners in order. Far more placid were the ducks and geese which wandered at will through the settlement just as you see them today."

The guards' voices are raised again in drunken laughter, and the coach pulls away leaving the scene in darkness.

SCENE TEN:
THE MINISTER'S HOUSE

It must be remembered that not all Commandants were fiends. Captain Maconochie was an early advocate, and practitioner, of prison reform; and there were the ministers, chaplains, call them what you will. It is incredibly difficult to understand how a man of God could tolerate fellow men being treated the way so many prisoners were on Norfolk Island. Some ministers did attempt to bring influence to bear with the authorities in New South Wales.

Opposite the tall Administration buildings on Quality Row is a simple house which was the residence of the Church of England minister at the time of the Penal Settlements. The Minister is standing on the covered porch in front of his home.

"What a soul destroying place this Norfolk Island is," he says. "When a prisoner arrives here he loses the heart of a man, and becomes a beast. And there are others, besides the prisoners, who need my spiritual guidance. The men – some with their wives – who have been posted to this forsaken isle are needed in the civilian trades. Behind the scenes you can find shoemakers, carpenters, glaziers, painters, cooks and blacksmiths quietly going about their daily work.

When Commandant Maconochie came in 1840, he was horrified to find that the convicts were habitually outraged and their self-respect destroyed. Knives and forks were not allowed at their tables. Instead, they tore at chunks of meat with their teeth, and grabbed food with their hands.

It was against this type of degradation that the Catholic priest and I had to work. We were only allowed to speak with the prisoners on Sunday mornings, unless a formal visit to the hospital or gaol cells had been arranged.

Our income was pitiful. All the clergy posted here had to survive on two hundred pounds a year, between us. That is the total sum that the New South Wales Church Act would allow for each mission post. Many of the officers were not fit to be caretakers of these poor wretches. Should I speak in judgment of such men? It tears my heart to see the rotten standards that were evident everywhere one looked. The moral misdeeds of the imprisoned men are looked on with amusement, and yet the slightest attitude of disrespect to the Military is given severe punishment.

I pray that there will be some enlightenment, and that the conditions will improve for these human beings so incarcerated.

God be with you, my people."

SCENE ELEVEN:
THE OLD BARRACKS

There's another tall building set in gracious grounds.

Dennis Doherty speaks. "Look over on your left. These soldiers are guarding the gates to the Old Barracks. All the officers were quartered here, unless they had wives and families with them. The swine were so fearful of us breaking out, guards were posted night and day over the cells."

The front courtyard of the Old Barracks is lit. There is an officer in military uniform walking along the path to the barrack steps. His voice can be heard as he indicates the high walls of the yard.

The officer speaks, "I was assigned to this post on Norfolk Island to control and discipline the convicts. But look at these walls that surround me. I feel just as much a prisoner as they.

The hands that have bled and blistered while erecting these buildings may be the hands of thieves and murderers, yet they are still men. The ghastly scenes that I have witnessed will burn in my memory forever.

I long for peace from this hell. Perhaps at the end of my term here I may have earned a land grant somewhere beyond Bathurst where I can till the soil. Only physical labour will help alleviate the mental torment."

Doherty: "The Old Barracks building has seen countless arguments over the years. It still does! You see, today it is the Assembly House, and the arguments continue."

SCENE TWELVE:
A DOMESTIC SCENE

The coach stops outside No. 9 Quality Row.

A woman in formal afternoon dress is standing on the front lawn with her daughter. The woman voices some of her thoughts. "It was strange here for the women on Norfolk Island. We couldn't help feeling sorry for the convicts at times, even though they had committed great offences against society.

Certainly, the prisoners' voices and bearing are rude and uncouth, and it gives us ladies who are wives of the officers a most uncomfortable feeling as their eyes follow us whenever we walk and ride through the settlement."

She continues, "There are young, brash men here, as well as older ones, who are sorely missing the female companionship and comfort that they were used to at Home."

The girl can see a ship approaching. "Look, Mama. There is a ship arriving from Sydney Town. Will it have the silk for my new dress?"
The woman looks at her fondly. "I hope so. There'll be a letter from your dear grandmama, too, my child."

The light fades.

SCENE THIRTEEN:
THE CEMETERY

Historic graves

Doherty resumes his story. "Let us pause and read some of the headstones in the cemetery. They are memorials to some of those who died in these ghastly penal settlements."

The spotlight shines to the right of the coach, and viewers can see over the fence to the gravestones in the Old Cemetery close to the beach.

Six voices will be heard. As if from the graves they come.

The first is that of a woman. "I am Widow Smith. My dear husband, Steven Smith, was a free overseer the night of the convict uprising at the Cookhouse in July 1846.

While he was on duty, he and three other constables were barbarously murdered by those devils. Now here I am alone, on this wretched island, a widow with three children and oh, how we pine for him."

Then a man's voice is heard. "My name is Thomas Salisbury Wright." And chuckling, "They say a leopard does not change its spots, nor a criminal his way of life. I was fully sixty years old when I was first convicted of forgery back in the County of York.

Much later, I was sentenced to transportation to Norfolk Island for printing my own bank notes." Chuckling again at the memory, he continues his story. "Well, at one hundred and two years of age I could hardly have been expected to survive the full term of my fourteen year prison sentence. So I rest in peace at last in Norfolk's soil."

Atkinson says, "I am John Atkinson. I died at the age of thirty-seven years. Before becoming a prisoner of the Crown I had seen better days, and Major Ryan recognised this. I was made Constable at Government House. I perished in the service of the Governor while I was out at sea one day, fishing for his supper."

Another woman speaks. "I am Susanna Pery. My dear husband, William, was one of the Commanding Officers on Norfolk Island. However, not long after arriving here we received word that he had inherited the title of Earl of Limerick. It was too late to return to Ireland; we were committed to the position he'd taken on Norfolk Island.

I loved William dearly, but it was difficult coming to the realisation that his appointment to this terrible place had taken me away from my usual domestic comforts. I died fifteen days after giving birth to our first, and therefore only child, a daughter, who was dead herself six months later; God bless her darling, little soul.

Mrs Core was the wife of a civilian worker at the settlement. She speaks now, as a voice from the dead. "I lost my children too, on this terrible island. Every mother in the world would feel for me in this isolated place to where I came to accompany my husband in his posting.

I had two children; George died when he was just two months old and Jane, who had helped take his place in our hearts, died the next year when she was only four months old."

There are men, women and children from the Penal Settlements buried in the cemetery on Norfolk Island. You can still visit their graves.

The scene finishes with a man's voice. "I am Private James Neale of the King's Own Regiment. I was accidentally shot when out hunting in the woods one day."

Doherty rejoins, "It's a mighty good thing that I had an alibi the day that Neale died, or I could have ended up on the gallows myself!"

The light shining over the cemetery fades, and the coach moves to the final scene.

SCENE FOURTEEN:
THE LEGEND OF BLOODY BRIDGE

The tour coach moves slowly round the cliff road towards the final terrible episode. It stops and turns to face Bloody Bridge – a wondrous piece of engineering over a narrow deep valley.

The road over Bloody Bridge

Strobe lighting is used during part of the ensuing scene to accentuate the frantic nature of this episode in Norfolk Island's history – one that cannot be entirely discounted.

Doherty tells the story: "Most of the convict overseers were hated by the men for they were often more cruel and rigorous than the soldiers. Many times the convict overseers would be attacked by the group working under their command, and sometimes they were murdered. Legend has it that such a thing happened at Bloody Bridge.

Listen! I hear Commandant Price approaching."

Price says, in his clipped tones, "Our new road past the cemetery will be the best way to reach Ball Bay. The route, though steep, is satisfactory on foot. But in winter we will never be able to ford that stream in the deep gully.
Take twelve convicts who are in irons, ones who will do a good job with pick and shovel – the best stone from Point Hunter will be required – and work them hard so that the bridge is ready for use before the April rains."

Sounds are heard: waves breaking on the rocky shore, men groaning, hammer and chisel on stone, the rattle of leg irons, curses from the overseer and a whip cracking, men screaming in pain and desperation.

Doherty resumes his account. "And so the work began. The ground in this area was unstable which presented the men with many a problem in keeping a foothold. The prisoners were chained together in pairs to prevent an easy escape. Nevertheless, they had to work on this new building project from daylight till dusk, with no breakfast. They had but one break in this long day, at noon, for a meagre lunch of corned meat and maize."

The overseer's voice breaks through. "Speed it up, you laggards. Come on! Lift that stone higher – higher – and fit it in with the others. You can reach. Reach! Haul those stones up." Rocks fall. "You cursed fools. The bridge should be finished by now. Move your bones, man, or I'll encourage you further with my stick."

A convict retaliates: "I'm working as hard as I can, damn you. If the Major would give us some decent food to fill our bellies we'd do better." Much good this reply will do him!

The overseer sneers, "That's not my problem. I want this wall finished today, else I'll have some of your names in report."

A second convicts speaks. "If ye weren't so keen on sending men off to the scourge, or solitary, we'd have more of them here to help us get the job done."

Overseer: "That's enough of your lip. You'll do as I say, and you'll do it now!"

The voice of yet another convict is now heard. "Curses! It's too hot for this kind of work. The gangs at Longridge have been given light duties these last three days 'cause of the heat. What about us?"

Second convict: "Strike me, would ye, ye black hearted villain? It was only three months ago ye were doing the same work as me. I'll not stomach orders from a dog like ye. Take that!"

He bashes the overseer with the handle of a pick and knocks him down. Then he strikes the tyrant repeatedly despite the fallen man's screams. Other convicts working on the bridge give bloodcurdling yells.

Doherty: "They set upon their overseer..."
The convicts emit a blood-curdling yell.
Doherty: "...All that pent-up hatred showed itself in full force."

Convict voices are raised above the melee.

"Attack!"
"Get him! We'll not take this any longer."
"Let 'im feel what the whip is like on 'is back."
"I'd like to do more than just whip 'im".

A gunshot rings out.

Doherty: "A gunshot means that one of the overseers is calling for reinforcements, but it will be too late for this man."

Other convicts join in, bashing the overseer with their shovels and picks. They appear to tip the body over the side of the bridge.

Doherty: "The convicts needed to hide the dead man, and quickly. They set to with feverish energy and walled up his body behind the brickwork. The dastardly deed was done.

When they returned to the settlement they said that the overseer had taken a walk along the cliffs, but never returned. Ha, ha!"

Doherty continues: "Soldiers from the camp went to investigate, and although they found the bridgework complete, they discovered the unmistakable trickle of human blood coming from between the bricks where the mortar had not set."

Looking down from the top of Bloody Bridge

The alleged assailants in this ghastly crime were rounded up and their trial held before Judge Feilding Brown the next morning. It was quite evident what their fate would be.

Feilding Brown speaks in judgement: "As His Majesty's Magistrate on this terrible Isle, I find all twelve of you guilty of wilful murder. At three o'clock this afternoon you shall be executed at the gallows. There will be no appeal."

Doherty is appalled. "The convicts were forced to dig a mass grave."

We hear the beat of a drum, and the resounding clang of the trap door twelve times as the gallows above does its dreadful work.

It is hoped that the souls of those twelve men are at rest now. You, the witnesses to this terrible episode at Bloody Bridge – modern day tourists - now leave the scene."

The coach moves back along Quality Row, and back to Burnt Pine.

Doherty has a final few words. "You have gone back in time to share these memories with me. Thank God it was never as bad in the Penal Settlement again. Commandant Price was removed in 1853.

Let me now return you to the present day. I pray to God in Heaven that we will never see the like again of what you have just witnessed. Yet, tragically such things are still happening somewhere in the world even today. You are the lucky ones. Let us hope that men will learn to be more tolerant of others and treat their fellow beings with greater compassion."

You who are visiting beautiful Norfolk Island will have experienced for yourselves the warm spirit and strong perseverance of the people of this peaceful island community.

Photographs of buildings at Kingston
are with the approval and consent
of the Norfolk Island Administration.

References:

The Journal of Ensign Best

Archaeological Survey of Kingston - Arthurs Vale,
     Wilson & Davies

Convicts and Commandants of Norfolk Island,
     Margaret Hazzard

Norfolk Island; A history through illustration,
     Merval Hoare

Cover design and layout by Bev Robitai
Photography by the author

www.ingramcontent.com/pod-product-compliance
Lightning Source LLC
Chambersburg PA
CBHW041429090426
42741CB00003B/94